T0195837

THE MEANING OF CHRISTMAS

A Savior is Born!

COURTNEY LITTLE

WestBow Press books may be ordered through booksellers or by contacting:

WestBow Press
A Division of Thomas Nelson & Zondervan
1663 Liberty Drive
Bloomington, IN 47403
www.westbowpress.com
844-714-3454

Interior Image Credit: Andy McGinnis

Scriptures taken from the Holy Bible, New International Version®, NIV®. Copyright © 1973, 1978, 1984, 2011 by Biblica, Inc.™ Used by permission of Zondervan. All rights reserved worldwide. www.zondervan.com The "NIV" and "New International Version" are trademarks registered in the United States Patent and Trademark Office by Biblica, Inc.®

ISBN: 978-1-6642-6494-6 (sc)
ISBN: 978-1-6642-6495-3 (e)

Library of Congress Control Number: 2022907705

Print information available on the last page.

WestBow Press rev. date: 5/5/2022

WESTBOW
PRESS®
A DIVISION OF THOMAS NELSON
& ZONDERVAN

ACKNOWLEDGEMENTS

Thank you to my husband, Tyler, for helping me to thoughtfully and carefully answer doctrinal questions and find scripture references.

Thanks to Pastor Tim for his expositional teaching of scripture, and his faithfulness in serving the Lord.

Thanks be to God, for giving me the ability and opportunity to proclaim the gospel message through a children's book, and for using me to accomplish His purposes.

"Mom, can we read a Christmas story before bed tonight?"

"Emmett, let's think for a minute about the meaning of Christmas, and about God's plan for an everlasting kingdom," Mom responded. "Before the beginning of time, God the Father, God the Son, and God the Holy Spirit made a plan."

"Like they had a meeting?" interjected Emmett.

"Well, I guess so," said Mom, "but they are one God, so they were always together. They are the Trinity."

"The Trinity?" asked Emmett.

"Yes. It's a mystery to us, but that is what the Bible teaches us about God. The Bible tells us they planned to design a creation. They would make time, energy, matter and life. They would make man in God's own image, and so they did. In the beginning, everything was perfect."

3

Mom continued, "But God knew that when He gave man the ability to make his own choices, that man would think he knew better than God, leading him to disobey and destroy the perfect relationship with God. That is what happened when Adam and Eve sinned in the Garden by eating the forbidden fruit. You see, God cannot allow sin in His presence, because He is holy. Do you know what sin is, Emmett?"

"When you disobey God?" answered Emmett.

"Yes. Sin is like a sickness that can't be cured. Even our best behaviors are stained by sin. When Adam and Eve introduced sin, a curse was placed on mankind so that we are born incapable of obeying God perfectly."

"We are under a curse?" asked Emmett.

"Yes, everyone dies as a result of sin. Do you know what God says is the punishment for sin?"

"Hell?" answered Emmett.

"That's right," said Mom. "The only way we can be in heaven with Jesus someday is by trusting in Him as the only acceptable sacrifice for our sin."

Emmett spoke up, "A sacrifice is when you kill something."

"That's right, said Mom. "God's plan was to send his Son to be born as a man so that He could die as a sacrifice for our sins. Otherwise, we have to be eternally separated from God, and without God's goodness and mercy, hell will be eternal sadness and torment."

"Mom, I have a question," said Emmett. "How can Jesus be both man and God?"

"Well," said Mom, "That's the mystery of the incarnation."

"Incarnation?" asked Emmett.

"Yes, Emmett, God in the flesh. He loves us so much that He was willing to give up all His privileges as God- all of His glory, honor, and riches to be born in this sin-cursed world so that He could die to take the punishment we deserve for our sin. He was the only person who never sinned and yet He died a painful, shameful, and lonely death on the cross because of His great love for us."

"Emmett, do you know how God became flesh?"

"The Holy Spirit put Him in Mary's belly," Emmett answered.

"Good job, Emmett," said Mom. "An Angel was sent to tell Mary that she was the chosen one to give birth to the savior of the world."

Emmett said, "She was going to name Him Jesus."

"Do you know what the name Jesus means?" asked Mom.

"No," said Emmett.

"It means 'God Saves'," said Mom. God sent another angel to Joseph in a dream to tell him he would be Mary's husband and would help raise Jesus."

"What happens next, Mom?" asked Emmett.

"Well, you tell me, Emmett," Mom said.

"Joseph and Mary had to take a long trip to Bethlehem to be counted," Emmett replied. "Mary was about to deliver Baby Jesus, but when they got to Bethlehem, they couldn't find a room in an inn. An Inn Keeper told them they could stay in his stable. Mary had Jesus and laid him in the manger."

"Do you know what a manger is, Emmett?"

"No, what?" responded Emmett.

"A manger is a feeding trough for the animals."

"Oh," said Emmett.

"Emmett, do you know why God planned for the savior of the world to be born in a manger?" Mom asked.

"Because it would be safe there?" Emmett responded.

"Actually, it was planned that way from the beginning of time because God wanted us to know that when Jesus gave up His kingship in heaven, it was to become a lowly servant on earth, obeying His Father even unto death," said Mom.

"Emmett, did you know that an angel appeared to shepherds, who were likely hired servants, to tell them the news about Jesus's birth? A whole bunch of angels appeared to them and praised God before them. The angel told them where to find baby Jesus."

"What about the wise men?" asked Emmett

"They were not servants. They were highly honored people from a faraway place. God uses all different kinds of people to accomplish His purposes, and He even put a special star in the sky to lead the wise men to Jesus after He was born. Talk about a grand plan!"

"Emmett, the Christmas story is amazing! It is about a savior coming into the world! Isn't that the best gift ever?"

"Yes!" answered Emmett.

"Emmett, do you know what Jesus wants for Christmas from you?"

"Love?" answered Emmett.

"Yes, answered Mom. "He wants you to love and obey Him. When we do that, it shows that we belong to Him. You see, when someone truly belongs to God, God begins to change that person to be more like Jesus- humble, selfless, and serving others out of love in obedience to His Father. Did we miss any important parts of the Christmas story, Emmett?" Mom asked.

"I think you got the important stuff, Mom," said Emmett.

23

"Ok Emmett. Next time we'll talk about how He died for us, and His resurrection and return to His throne in Heaven, but that is the Easter story, so we'll save that for later," Mom said.

"Love you, Mom."

"Love you too, Emmett. Good night, buddy. Sweat dreams."

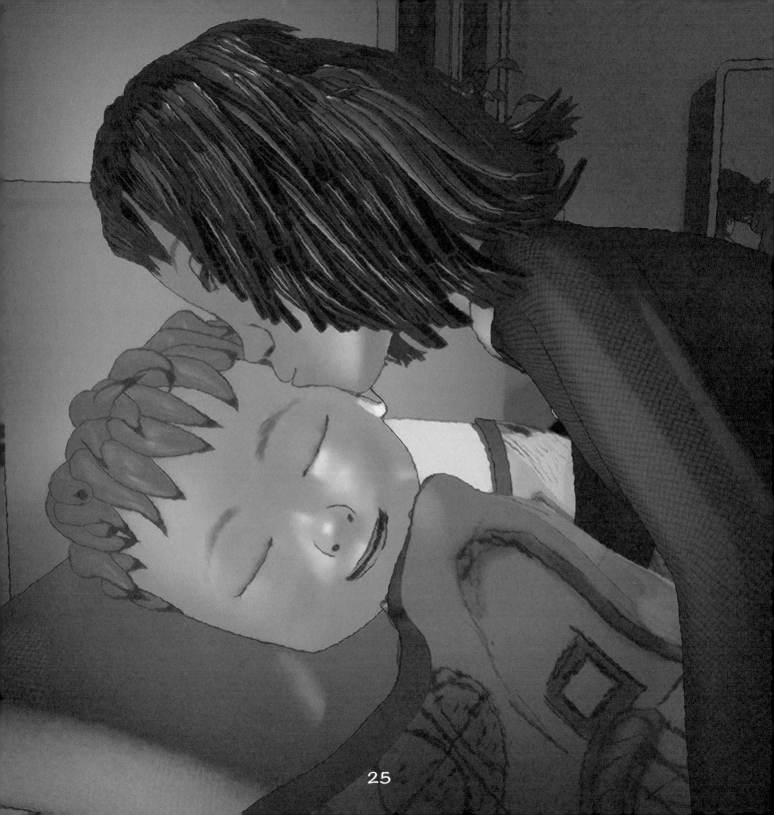

Going Deeper: Scripture references to Emmett's questions

1. Why did God create man?

   Isaiah 43:7 Everyone who is called by my name, whom I created for my glory, whom I formed and made.

   Romans 11:36 For from him and through him and for him are all things. To him be the glory forever! Amen.

   Revelation 4:11 You are worthy, our Lord and God, to receive glory and honor and power, for you created all things, and by your will they were created and have their being.

2. Who is the Trinity?

   Genesis 1:26 Then God said, "Let **us** make mankind in our image, in **our** likeness..."

   Deuteronomy 6:4 Hear, O Israel: The LORD our God, the LORD is one.

   Matthew 28:19 Therefore go and make disciples of all nations, baptizing them in the name of the Father and of the Son and of the Holy Spirit

   John 1:1-3 In the beginning was the Word, and the Word was with God, and the Word was God. He was with God in the beginning. Through him all things were made; without him nothing was made that has been made.

John 14:16-17 And I will ask the Father, and he will give you another advocate to help you and be with you forever—the Spirit of Truth

1 Peter 1:2 who have been chosen according to the foreknowledge of God the Father, through the sanctifying work of the Spirit, to be obedient to Jesus Christ and sprinkled with his blood: Grace and peace be yours in abundance.

3. What is the incarnation?

Matthew 1:23 The virgin will conceive and give birth to a son, and they will call him Immanuel (which means "God with us").

John 1:14 The Word became flesh and made His dwelling among us. We have seen His glory, the glory of the one and only Son, who came from the Father, full of grace and truth.

Philippians 2:5-8 In your relationships with one another, have the same mindset as Christ Jesus: Who, being in very nature God, did not consider equality with God something to be used to his own advantage; rather, he made himself nothing by taking the very nature of a servant, being made in human likeness. And being found in appearance as a man, He humbled Himself by becoming obedient to death— even death on a cross!

4. What is sin?

Jeremiah 17:9 The heart is deceitful above all things and beyond cure. Who can understand it?

Romans 3:23 for all have sinned and fall short of the glory of God

Romans 5:12 Therefore, just as sin entered the world through one man, and death through sin, and in this way death came to all people, because all sinned

1 John 2:16-17 For everything in the world- the lust of the flesh, the lust of the eyes, and the pride of life- comes not from the Father but from the world. The world and its desires pass away, but whoever does the will of God lives forever.

1 John 3:4 Everyone who sins breaks the law; in fact, sin is lawlessness.

5. What is the punishment for sin?

Genesis 3:17-19 To Adam he said, "Because you listened to your wife and ate fruit from the tree about which I commanded you, 'You must not eat from it,' "Cursed is the ground because of you; through painful toil you will eat food from it all the days of your life. It will produce thorns and thistles for you, and you will eat the plants of the field. By the sweat of your brow you will eat your food until you return to the ground, since from it you were taken; for dust you are and to dust you will return."

John 3:36 Whoever believes in the Son has eternal life, but whoever rejects the Son will not see life, for God's wrath remains on them.

Romans 6:23 For the wages of sin is death, but the gift of God is eternal life in Christ Jesus our Lord.

Revelation 21:8 But the cowardly, the unbelieving, the vile, the murderers, the sexually immoral, those who practice magic arts, the idolaters and all liars—they will be consigned to the fiery lake of burning sulfur. This is the second death.

6. Why did Jesus have to die as a sacrifice for our sins?

Isaiah 53:12b For he bore the sin of many, and made intercession for the transgressors.

Ephesians 1:7 In him we have redemption through his blood, the forgiveness of sins, in accordance with the riches of God's grace

Ephesians 2:8-9 For it is by grace you have been saved, through faith—and this is not from yourselves, it is the gift of God— not by works, so that no one can boast.

1 Peter 3:18 For Christ also suffered once for sins, the righteous for the unrighteous, to bring you to God. He was put to death in the body but made alive in the Spirit.

1 John 2:2 He is the atoning sacrifice for our sins, and not only for ours but also for the sins of the whole world.

7. How do you know you are saved and belong to God?

John 14:15 If you love me, keep my commands.

Ephesians 4:22-24 You were taught, with regard to your former way of life, to put off your old self, which is being corrupted by its deceitful desires; to be made new in the attitude of your minds; and to put on the new self, created to be like God in true righteousness and holiness.

1 John 2:5-6 But if anyone obeys his word, love for God is truly made complete in them. This is how we know we are in him: Whoever claims to live in him must live as Jesus did.

1 John 3:9-10 No one who is born of God will continue to sin, because God's seed remains in them; they cannot go on sinning, because they have been born of God. This is how we know who the children of God are and who the children of the devil are: Anyone who does not do what is right is not God's child, nor is anyone who does not love their brother and sister.

Printed in the United States
by Baker & Taylor Publisher Services